Looking at Music

Ian Fenton

CRANE, RUSSAK & COMPANY INC.,
347 Madison Avenue
New York, N.Y. 10017

© Ian Fenton 1977
First published in the U.S.A. by
Grane, Russak & Company Inc.
Library of Congress number 77 83148
ISBN 0 8448 1269 2

Introduction

Music is an unsolved mystery. There is music all around us in rock groups, dance music, folk music, classical concerts, opera, and from many different types of solo singers and instrumentalists. We can listen to it any time 'live', or in the privacy of our own rooms on radio, TV, records or cassettes. Anyone can learn to play any instrument, there are private teachers everywhere, and music is also taught in schools. There are many books on musical history, composition and appreciation. Music is a very big part of the lives of some of us, and all of us respond to it at some level. Yet in spite of all this, we still don't really know why; and that is the unsolved mystery of music.

People in ancient times were very much more awed by this mystery than we are. Music was considered to be a gift from the gods, and was an important part of religious ceremonies and healing.

Perhaps no one has been as near to solving the mystery of the 'why' of music than was the school of Pythagoras, the Greek thinker who lived over two thousand years ago.

His understanding of music was part of his mathematical understanding of man and of the whole universe. Some of this forms the basis of our modern study of geometry, and we have all heard of one small part of it in Pythagoras' *theorem*. Although the exact mathematical workings of his musical understanding have been lost, we do know now that one of the bases of music's meaning to us is mathematical. We talk about this later in the book, as well as about the modern instruments which demonstrate it.

Pythagoras realized that everything was connected to everything else, or was in relationship to it. He used the relationship of distances between the sun, moon and planets and the earth as a basis for musical notes. He found that when he scaled down these distances into strings of different lengths, attached at both ends, he could pluck the strings and make harmonious sounds.

It is thought that from his model of the 'music of the spheres' he and his followers became convinced that the different sounds represented by the seven strings were the basic scale (from the Latin, *scala*, a ladder) of music.

There is a fairly common accord that our musical scales in the West came from Greek scales, whether from Pythagoras or not. Music is made around five-note, seventeen-note and many other types of scale in different parts of the world. We should remember, however, that music is made first, and only afterwards come the attempts to define it. Is there a relationship between ourselves, music and the whole cosmos, as Pythagoras believed? Some of us may feel there is. Others will perhaps look to quantum physics and mathematics for the answer.

Just as music is the organising of random sounds, we had better organise some of the thoughts that we have already touched on, making them parts of this book so that we can deal with them in more detail. This, then, might make an interesting list of contents.

What is music?
Sound; instruments; structure; notation and techniques; the effect on the mind and the feelings; music and the cosmos.

Basic sounds or types
Eastern and western; African; folk; military; synthetic and computer music.

Music through the ages
Early music; the Renaissance and royal patronage; the Golden Age; opera; Baroque, Classical and Romantic; 20th Century music; Musical comedy; popular music today.

The deeper meaning of music
The meaning of the composer's gift; personal taste in music.

Conclusion

Men used to believe that all power in their lives was held by the Gods and Goddesses. Those who were thought to be the source of the arts were called Muses, all daughters of the great God Zeus.

From this we see the origin of the word music, whose own muse was Euterpe, or if dance is included, Terpsichore.

What is music ?

Music is sound organised in a way which is interesting for our minds and which affects our feelings. Sound is waves in the air which, although we can't see them, are very much like waves in water. These 'sound waves' affect our ears by bouncing off a tight membrane in the ear, called the eardrum. This movement is then transmitted through the nerve channels to the brain.

Thousands of waves arrive at our ears every second from each source of sound. Our ears respond to them and our brains interpret them. Yet the only ones which have that pleasurable quality of musicality are those organised rhythmically and having a regular frequency or vibration making a definite pitch.

5

Some very unusual and simple organisations of rhythmic sound can be music. For instance, try gently striking glasses filled with different levels of water, or blow air through a piece of tissue paper wrapped round a comb. If you have a tape recorder, try recording fragments of everyday sounds and then play them back as one continuous sound. Some very exhilarating music has come from kitchen or 'jug' bands in some parts of America, where people get together with washing boards, tissue covered combs, kitchen pans and other such 'instruments' and make music. Some people can get tunes out of flexing an ordinary wood saw.

An easily improvised musical instrument from milk bottles. Adjust water level for pitch required.

It's easy to see how the brain, and therefore possibly the mind, is involved in the interpretation of music. But it is important also to realize that a quality of music is its ability to affect our feelings. People can be moved to tears, to laughter, and to intense happiness by music. Whole nations can be made to feel proud. Think of the stirring military music you have heard, and what that must have meant to the regiments for whom it was written and played when they were marching into battle.

We also see that music reflects the life and times of the people who made and played it. Listen for the pomp and gaiety in the music which emerged from the colourful royal courts of 18th- and 19th-century Europe. Feel the devotion of the early Church plain-song, the vigour and rhythmic impetus of Cossack or African music, or the hypnotic affect of Buddhist chanting. Particularly if you ever have the chance, listen to a contempory rendering of the temple music of ancient Egypt, like that composed by Dennis Stoll to accompany his temple dancers. This music and dance has a healing effect which only deepens the mystery of music.

So we have begun to paint a picture of what music is by looking at its qualities, and the way it is made. We know it has to be *organised* sound. We know it can come from any source. We know it can affect our minds and our feelings, and we know that it reflects something of the life and times of the people who made and played it. It involves *relationship*, between composer and player, player and listener, and sounds to each other. And as we saw at the beginning with Pythagoras' model, it probably involves our relationship as living rhythmic bodies with the living rhythmic universe around us.

The Music of the Spheres — a subject for speculation.

Instruments

Let us now look at some of the instruments of making music. Sound waves can be set in motion by three main groups of instruments. With *strings*, by plucking, striking or drawing a bow across gut nylon or metal "strings". With *wind*, by air being blown out of a tube. With *percussion*, by striking an object like a drum or cymbal.

In order to produce different frequencies (faster for higher notes and slower for lower notes), we need to be able to lengthen and shorten the vibrated parts of instruments and they are designed for the player's hands to vary these lengths.

You can demonstrate the relationship between length and frequency of vibration by taking a piece of elastic and stretching it to its fullest, plucking it and listening to the high sound and then relaxing it and listening to the lower sound it gives when plucked.

The earliest instrument we know of is the lyre, which was reputed in the legends to have been invented by Mercury, the god of craftsmen, who gave it to Apollo, the god of the sun, as appeasement when Mercury was caught stealing Apollo's cattle. The first picture of the lyre in real history was found in an Egyptian tomb, whose occupant probably heard its melody some 3400 years ago.

One of the most complex "instruments" of all, which existed even before the lyre, is the human voice. The sounds come from the "strings" or *vocal chords* in our throats vibrating against a column of air breathed out from the lungs and thus producing the sound waves common to all music. Singers of classical music or opera are usually classified by the range of music they can sing, such as bass, tenor and alto for men and contralto and soprano for women. Pop singers are known more by the type of music they sing like blues, rock or folk.

Strings

Among the strings are the violin, viola, guitar, cello, zither, sitar, bass, banjo, ukelele, harpsichord and piano. Pianos are also percussion instruments, as the strings are struck rather than plucked to make them vibrate. Strings normally seem to play the emotional role in the orchestra. Nothing can sound so happy as a ukelele, or so sad and yearning as a violin. Violins have a very wide range or distance between their top and bottom notes, as wide in fact as the range of human emotions they are often called upon to portray.

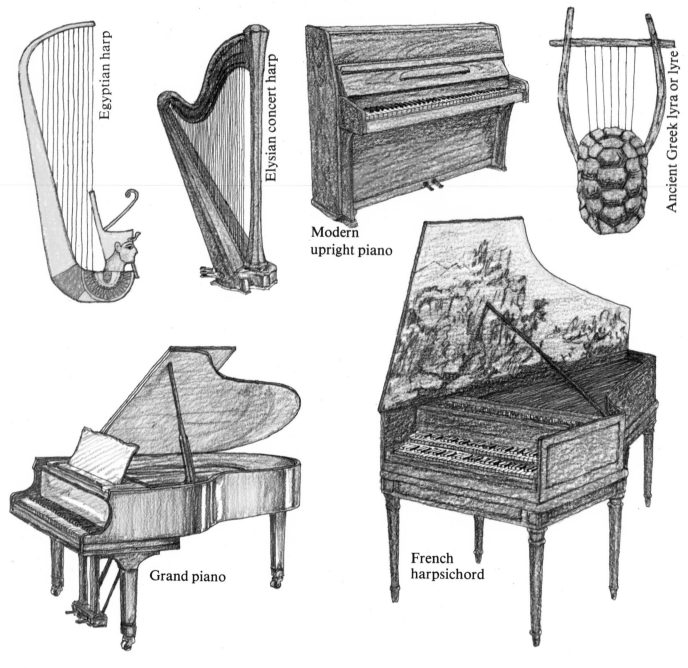

Egyptian harp

Elysian concert harp

Modern upright piano

Ancient Greek lyra or lyre

Grand piano

French harpsichord

Northern Indian sitar

Russian balalaika

Renaissance lute

Spanish classical guitar

Fiddle

Double-neck electric guitar

Ukelele

Banjolele

Autoharp zither

Violin

Cello

Double bass

Tromba marine viol

11

Wind

Wind instruments are usually divided into *brass* and *woodwind*. Brass instruments, such as the trumpet, trombone, tuba, French horn, saxophone, cornet and euphonium, have a bright, clear sound which makes us think of the gaiety and substance of everyday life. Woodwind instruments, such as the clarinet, flute, piccolo, bassoon, oboe and English horn, have a sweeter, more mysterious sound which touches a deeper, more reflective part of us.

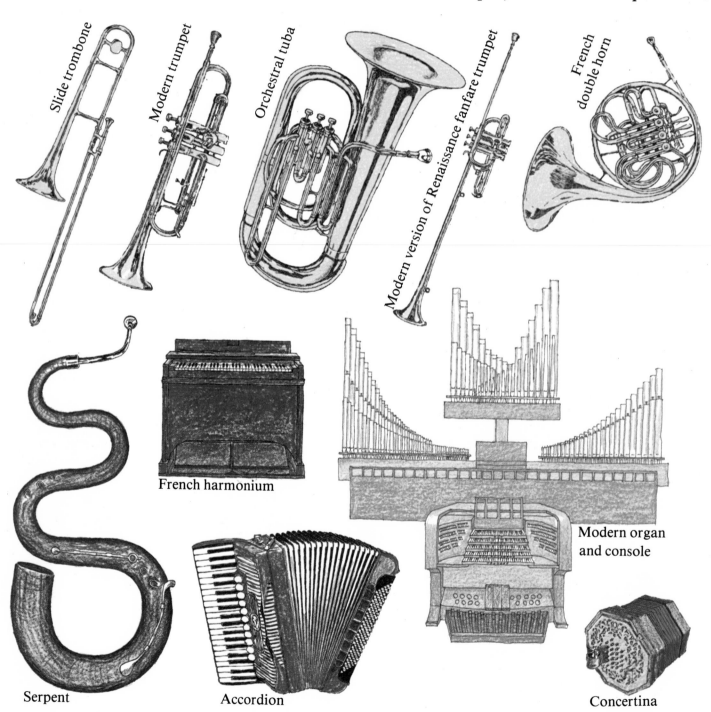

Slide trombone

Modern trumpet

Orchestral tuba

Modern version of Renaissance fanfare trumpet

French double horn

French harmonium

Modern organ and console

Serpent

Accordion

Concertina

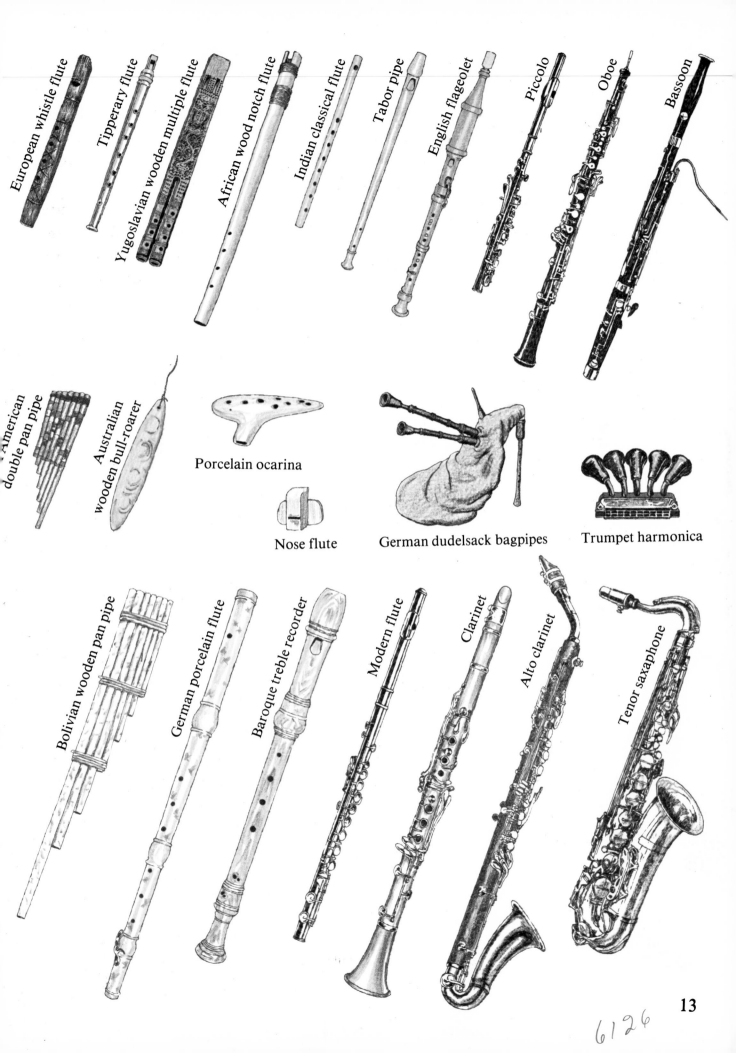

European whistle flute

Tipperary flute

Yugoslavian wooden multiple flute

African wood notch flute

Indian classical flute

Tabor pipe

English flageolet

Piccolo

Oboe

Bassoon

American double pan pipe

Australian wooden bull-roarer

Porcelain ocarina

Nose flute

German dudelsack bagpipes

Trumpet harmonica

Bolivian wooden pan pipe

German porcelain flute

Baroque treble recorder

Modern flute

Clarinet

Alto clarinet

Tenor saxaphone

13

6126

Percussion

Among the percussion instruments are the drum, cymbals, triangle, xylophone and chimes. Percussion instruments were probably played on their own first of all, much as we hear them today in drum solos. In modern music, drums set the rhythm or give the beat for the entire group or orchestra. This is as essential to music as the heartbeat is to life, or the planetary cycles are to the universe. It may well be that some of the more compelling rhythms of music are exactly in tune with those of the organs of our bodies. There has been very little research on this, although an interesting record has been made of the rhythms that we all hear in the womb before we are born. It sounds strangely like the rhythms of modern rock music.

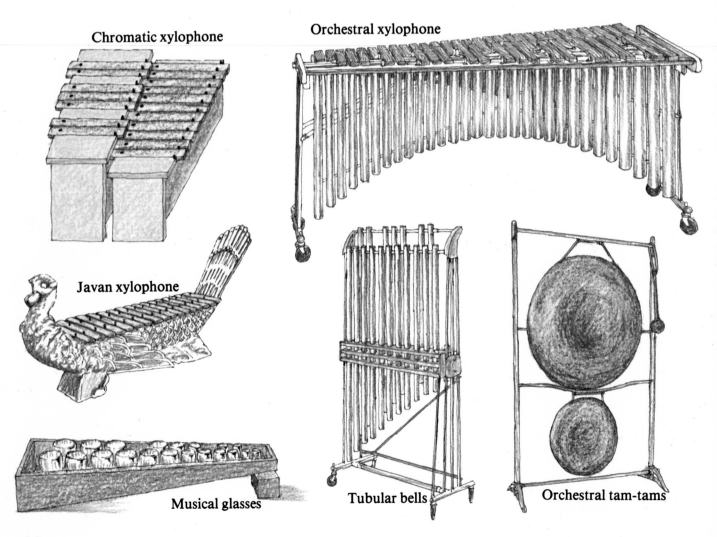

Chromatic xylophone

Orchestral xylophone

Javan xylophone

Musical glasses

Tubular bells

Orchestral tam-tams

Each of the three groups of instruments has its very own distinct sound, yet each group and each instrument within the group is still absolutely an individual. The skill of using an instrument is to give the greatest individual performance while keeping in tune and balance with the other instruments of the group and the orchestra. Once again, this is a bit like life, isn't it?

You can hear all the instruments of the orchestra taking part like actors in a play in Prokofiev's 'Peter and the Wolf', or Benjamin Britten's 'A Young Person's Guide to the Orchestra'.

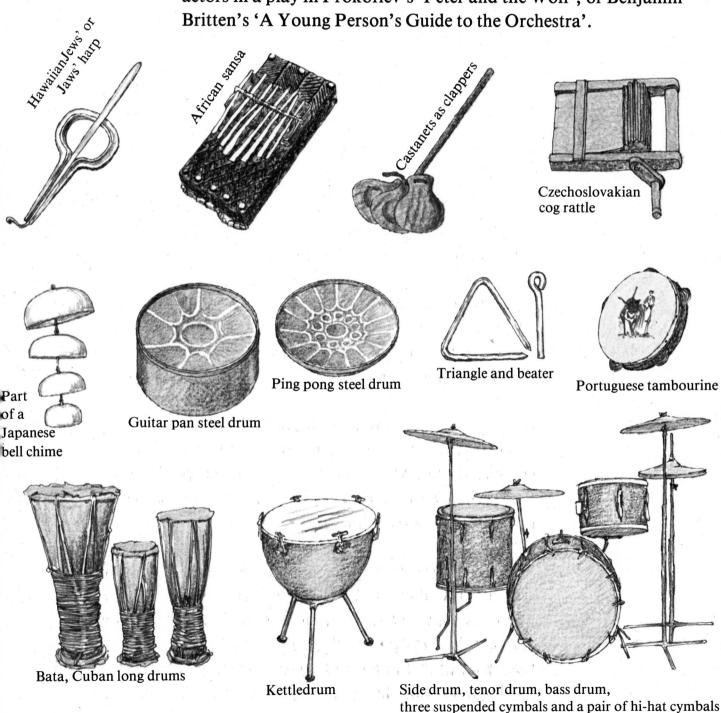

Hawaiian Jews' or Jaws' harp

African sansa

Castanets as clappers

Czechoslovakian cog rattle

Part of a Japanese bell chime

Guitar pan steel drum

Ping pong steel drum

Triangle and beater

Portuguese tambourine

Bata, Cuban long drums

Kettledrum

Side drum, tenor drum, bass drum, three suspended cymbals and a pair of hi-hat cymbals

Structure, notation and techniques

An oscilloscope. On the cathode ray tube display is a sound waveform. It is in constant movement, responding visually and instantly to the sound wave it is picking up.

We talk of human beings reaching heights of achievement and descending to depths of despair, and music has to reach as high and as low. The distance between the two is called *range*, and each instrument has a different range according to its construction. The exact degree of highness or lowness is called *pitch*. As the composer has to note down this exact pitch for it to be reproduced on an instrument, this is one use of the term note.

A high pitch we know is produced by faster or more frequent sound waves, and a lower pitch by a slower frequency. We can actually see this on an instrument called an *oscilloscope*.
You will see how remarkably like the waves of the ocean the note shown in the diagram looks.

If we take the seven steps or notes of Western music and add an eighth to join them to the next seven above, we have an *octave* (from the Latin, *octo*, meaning eight.) Here we have interesting mathematical support of Pythagoras' original theory in that the frequency of two notes, one octave apart, is such that the higher one is exactly double the lower one; and is in harmony with it.

Three or more notes struck together make a *chord*. Chords can be either harmonious or discordant, and our ears can tell us the difference. Harmonious or *harmonic* chords are pleasing to the ear, though only harmonic chords in music might be boring.

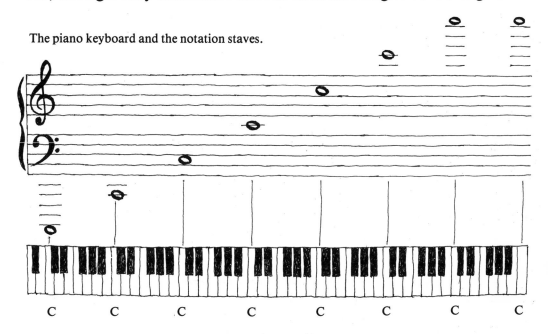

The piano keyboard and the notation staves.

The *key* in music serves the same function as the key to get into your house — it is simply the entry point, or starting point, of a musical scale. If you are playing a piece of music written in the key of C, it means that the basic scale of seven notes (which are indicated by the first seven letters of the alphabet) is the octave beginning and ending with C.

The whole composition will then relate to this note and its octave. There are major and minor versions of keys, each with its own distinct sound. These variations are achieved by raising with sharps (♯) or lowering with flats (♭) one or more notes in the key.

As music takes place in time, we need to know the order of the notes, the length of time we hold them, and *measures* or groupings of notes as well as flats and sharps, and other such symbols. So we have an arrangement of five parallel lines called a *stave* on which we write our notes, in the order in which they should be played. There are enough lines in a stave to show the notes in one octave. By adding other little lines (*ledger* lines) above and below the stave, we can also show where notes in different octaves have to be played — as in the diagram below. The staves have vertical bar lines along them at fixed intervals with a *time signature* at the beginning to show how many beats to a bar.

Notes are shown as blobs on or between the lines of the stave, and from the shape we know the note's duration in time. (See the diagram.) When you buy a simple teach yourself music book, or when you are taught by someone, you will soon learn and remember all the lines in the stave, as well as all the other building blocks of musical notation, structure and technique.

A skilled musician, by using all the elements and techniques we have talked about, can create an infinite number of effects. For instance, an easy one to listen for is the change of key from major to minor which can give music a sad and yearning sound — like parts of Beethoven's 'Moonlight Sonata'. However, we can still appreciate complicated music even without long study of its elements because it affects our feelings. And feeling music is equally important to listening to it with the mind.

The types of music which can be produced by the different cultures, ages and stages of development of man can be roughly classified — so let's now take a look at this.

The basic sounds of music

We have already talked a little about Western and Eastern music.
Eastern music lacks a single recognisable melody. This perhaps
relates to the fact that in most of the East, man regards himself as
part of a religion, a nation or a movement, but rarely regards
himself as being separate from other people as we do in the West.

Ravi Shankar playing sitar with Yehudi Menuhin playing violin.

Eastern religious music has a meditative quality about it, and
through meditation Eastern man gets in touch with his God and
the universe. Perhaps some Westerners need this too as Eastern
music is becoming more popular in the West, like the records of
Ravi Shankar playing his sitar.

Western music is also enjoying enormous popularity in the East.
Perhaps this means that some Easterners feel a need for the
greater self-expression of modern Western music.
Some musicians, like George Harrison, have tried to combine
East and West. In his album 'Living In the Material World', he
uses Eastern instrumentation and scales.

Go to your local record library and borrow some records of
traditional Indian, Chinese and Japanese music, and see what you
think and feel about them. Compare these to the inspiring
oratorios and masses of Bach, Mozart and Handel and to the
calmness of Gregorian chants, which are also a meditative music
intended to put man in touch with God.

Another basic sound is primitive African music. It underpins all of today's popular music. Compare it to rock music like that of the Rolling Stones. This music needs to be experienced in the body. Folk music also seems to have a distinct sound, even though it reflects the different lives and feelings of people in different parts of the world. Listen for the gaiety of peasant life in music like Morris dances, barn dances, and square dances, or for the passionate rhythms of Spanish Flamenco. How does military music make you feel? It has a similar sound whatever age or country it comes from. Can you hear pomp, pride, courage and aggression in Schubert's 'Marche Militaire'? Which instruments seem to you to echo these traits of human character?

Two new sounds of music are emerging now, which at first don't seem to be related to the life of man: computer music and synthetic music. But if we look at them carefully, we see that they too have a relationship to our lives and our world. Synthetic music is reproduced by electronic instruments. This may be music written for other instruments, or for a special electronic machine called a synthesiser. But the music is composed by man. One of the most interesting examples, easily obtainable, is music by Bach played on the Moog synthesiser.

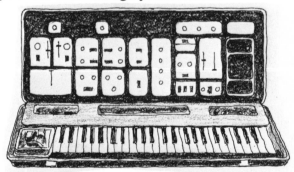

The Moog Synthesiser.

Computer music is composed and played by non-human means. But remember that a computer is only a rather simple model of some of the functions of the human brain. Look for comparisons with human composition. As computers don't have feelings to express, your emotions might not respond; but you may enjoy it anyway! Pierre Boulez is a name associated with this kind of music, and there are records by him which will be easy to get from your local record shop or library.

Music through the ages

Early Music

When we look at the history of music, we begin to see very quickly that what we are really looking at is the history of man. Music echoes the development of man, from the stage of using very simple tools and language, to the complexity of modern times. The first percussion instruments of ancient days were perhaps drums, which were used to pass messages from tribe to tribe or to stir man into the frenzy he needed to go to war with his neighbouring tribe. The early wind instruments were probably animal horns and sea shells, used to sound warning or to call cattle. The early stringed instruments, one of which, the lyre, we have already mentioned, may have been played to Kings or Gods.

We can imagine that the first real musicians were in great demand by their tribes or their rulers because their skill was regarded as something of a miracle. With so few means of enhancing the sparse life of those days, music must have seemed as amazing as colour television does now. No wonder that it was thought to be a gift from the gods!

Between the time of the fall of the Roman Empire in the fifth century A.D. and the Renaissance in the 16th century, there were two kinds of music: secular and sacred. Secular music (the music of the ordinary people) was sung, played and danced for pleasure, and was rarely written down. It often dealt with the subject of love, and has changed very little since that time — we can still hear traces of these early melodies in modern folk music.

Sacred music (music devoted to God) was very carefully structured by the Church, and was at first sung only by human voices. With the invention of printing in the 15th century, written music was able to be distributed to the common man, and secular and sacred music began to merge.

The Renaissance and Royal Patronage

Renaissance means rebirth, and at this time it really seemed as if

J. Sebastian Bach

cultural life and thought and learning had been reborn. Music and musicians too left the shadow of the Dark Ages. Some new instruments were invented, and musical forms began to change. Madrigals, the pop songs of the day, and dance music led the way out of the Dark Ages for secular music.

Just as the Popes and Church had been patrons of most of the written music of the Middle Ages, royalty and nobility became the patrons of music after the Renaissance. A patron (from the Latin, *pater*, meaning father) provided support and encouragement. Royalty allowed their musicians greater freedom to play and compose what they wanted, and they generally paid them. Musicians then, as today, were not always satisfied with the pay for their talents, and it's very interesting to read what some of the great musicians had to say about their patrons.

The Golden Age of Music
The Baroque period, from 1600 to 1750 saw a blossoming out of forms, textures, tonality, rhythm, dramatic styles and even types of instruments.

Handel

The musical sound is rich, joyful and full of vitality. Among the great names of the period were Bach, Handel, Telemann, Couperin, Corelli, Lully, Monteverdi, Scarlatti and Pachelbel. Some pieces typical of that period are those in Bach's 'Well Tempered Clavier', the immortal 'Canon' of Pachelbel, Corelli's 'Trio Sonatas' and Scarlatti's one-movement sonatas. Larger works typical of the period are Handel's 'Water Music' and Vivaldi's 'Four Seasons'.

Although opera really flowered during the later Romantic period, its beginnings were in the Baroque period with the work of such composers as Monteverdi, Lully, and Handel.

The Classical Period
From 1700 to the early 1800's music developed a balance which reminded people of the beauty and proportions of classical Greek art and architecture. Good examples are the symphonies of

Ludwig van Beethoven.

Johannes Brahms

Mozart

Frederic Chopin

Haydn, Mozart and most of those of Beethoven, such as Haydn's 'London Symphony' and Mozart's 'Jupiter' Symphony.
The operas of Mozart and Gluck led the way out of this period.

The Romantic Period

From the 1800's composers expressed their feelings and individuality with greater freedom, and the differences between their works could be clearly heard. Some of the composers of this period were Grieg, Schumann, Mendelssohn, Smetana, Dvorak, Borodin, Albeniz, Granados, Liszt, Brahms, Wagner, Weber, Chopin, Berlioz, Rimsky-Korsakov, Tchaikovsky, and the great opera composers like Verdi, Puccini, Mascagni, and Rossini, Wagner and Strauss.

Orchestras grew in size. Many new and varied instruments appeared, like the piano, and superb violins were made by craftsmen families around Cremona in Italy, among other places. One of them was the famous Stradivari family.

Great performers like Paganini and Caruso were known across the widening world of music. With better world transport, people were able to travel to listen and perform, so that the world of music became closer and more in touch with itself.

There are really no typical works of this period. However, as examples of it reflecting the increasing complexity of the life of the times, we could select the Italian operas of Verdi with their stirring melodies and their concern with political and social issues. We might also select the sophisticated ballet music of Tchaikovsky, such as 'Swan Lake', or the strength and colour of Borodin's 'Prince Igor'. Perhaps the most romantic music of the Romantic period is the piano music of Chopin.

The Twentieth Century

Many of the earlier trends of music still influenced the music of 1900 and onwards, although the forms were different.
Some of the great names bridging the 19th and 20th centuries are Mahler, Strauss, Sibelius, Debussy and Elgar. Stravinsky, Gershwin, Ravel, Copeland, Schoenberg, Bartok, Britten and Prokofiev are more truly of this century. Mahler's music can be

23

Franz Schubert

Paganini.

Giuseppe Verdi

heard in Ken Russell's film 'Mahler', which portrays the story of the composer's life. Other interesting examples of music from this period are Prokofiev's 'Peter and the Wolf', Schoenberg's 'Sprechtstimme', George Gershwin's 'Rhapsody in Blue', Stravinsky's 'The Rite of Spring', Ravel's 'Bolero', and the works of Stockhausen.

Musical Comedy

Musical comedy began in the twentieth century with works like Gilbert & Sullivan's 'Mikado', Franz Lehar's 'Merry Widow', Le Coq's 'La Fille de Madam Angot', and Offenbach's 'Orpheus in the Underworld'. The middle period of musicals, as they were soon called, saw works like Romberg's 'The Student Prince', Jerome Kern's 'Showboat' with lyrics by Rodgers and Hammerstein — who later produced 'South Pacific' and 'Oklahoma' — Irving Berlin's 'Annie Get Your Gun', Gershwin's 'Porgy and Bess', Bernstein's 'West Side Story', and in our own decade, 'Hair'.

Popular Music

Our present musical age is the pop age. Pop comes from the Latin word *populus*, which means people, and pop is truly the music of the people. It is mainly improvised — composed and played all at the same time. The jazz, blues, rock, folk, reggae and dance music of this age is the beat of our bodies and of the diversity of life around us. Our response to it draws us together. It even produces new cultures, with pop star leaders and prophets, though we should not forget that it is the individuality and musical originality of the stars which is being worshipped, at least in the beginning.

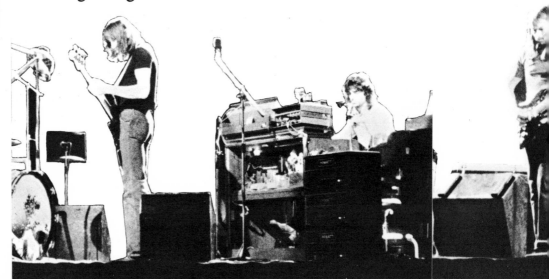

Elvis.

Pop lyrics often make statements about people and nations which have a common sense we can all learn from. Listen to Bob Dylan's 'The Times They Are A'Changin' or Joan Baez' 'Birmingham Sunday'. The poetic symbolism of pop lyrics paints in a few words what a psychology textbook tries to do in hundreds of pages. Listen to the Beatles' 'Eleanor Rigby' or 'Maxwell Silver Hammer'. Most of the energy of these lyrics goes into love, which is not a bad place for energy to go — as in the Beatles' 'I Wanna Hold Your Hand', 'Michelle', 'Girl' or the Rolling Stones' ''Let's Spend the Night Together'.

The roots of pop music lie in Africa and the East. The flowering is in America, stemming from the gospel and blues music of the Afro-Americans. To understand its roots, is to touch on a vision of a humanity as integrated, warm and alive as the music.

The Pink Floyd in concert.

Composers, performers and performances

We have only looked very briefly at some of the great names of each musical period as we have passed through the ages of music because space is limited. But there are good musical dictionaries in which most composers' and performers' names and lives can be found. Among the more complete is *Grove's Dictionary of Music and Musicians*.

What does a composer really do? Basically he is a channel, a gifted individual who in some way is in touch with his fellow men and with the cycles of life around him. He is able to organize his awareness and communicate it musically to his listeners. He puts us in touch with nature. He is doing by his composing what Pythagoras was trying to do in making his scale model of the solar system in the form of a musical instrument with strings. He is communicating the music of the spheres.

Because everyone is different, there will undoubtedly be particular composers, performers and types of music which will attract you more than others. The personal element is very important, because it helps to define who you are. Some opera lovers may only want to listen to operas starring Maria Callas in the female lead. Some piano lovers may find their greatest joy in Alfred Brendel's interpretation of Beethoven's piano music, or Arthur Rubenstein's interpretation of Chopin. Others will become collectors of rare interpretations like those of Dinu Lippatti, whose unusual brilliance ended in his death through leukaemia at the very young age of thirty-three. The solo cello interpretations of Emanuel Feurmann, another genius who died young, are still often regarded as the cellist's choice. Some of you may become hooked on Haifitz as the definitive interpretor of Beethoven's violin music, and others may stoutly defend the equal but different brilliance of the Belgian violinist Arthur Grumiaux. Develop your musical knowledge through what pleases you. The more we know this, the more we know about ourselves.

Other great names of this century are Schnabel, Horowitz, Rostropowitz, Cassals, Menuhin, and Toscanini. Perhaps you might be interested in finding out what this last small list of people did in the world of music.

In jazz, blues and ragtime composer and performer are often one and the same. Some of the great jazz musicians include the late Duke Ellington, Louis Armstrong, Charlie (Yardbird) Parker, Dizzy Gilespie, Count Basie, Glen Miller and the Dorsey brothers.

Modern jazz owes much to people like John Coltrane, Miles Davis, Thelonius Monk and the mellow tones of the Modern Jazz Quartet. In blues the development is led by Huddie Ledbetter (better known as Leadbelly), Blind Lemon Jefferson and Bessie Smith. Some of the more recent singers are Cleo Lane, BB King and Freddie King. Ragtime developed with Scott Joplin, Jelly Roll Morton and Fats Waller.

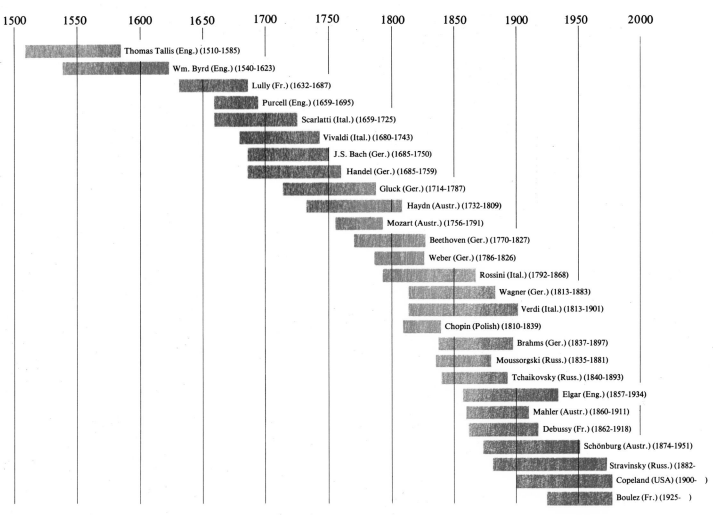

The great composers. Who could have talked to whom?

Conclusion

Now that we have organised our thoughts about music, just as music itself is the result of organising sound, we can learn to play an instrument, go to concerts, join local record libraries and begin really living our lives with music. We can seek out the types and the periods of music that we like.

We can also begin to look at the mystery of the 'why' of music, for answers to this age-old mystery. Why do you think music is an integral part of our world? Why does it have the same mathematical basis as electronics and physics? Could it relate to the fabric of the entire cosmos? Why do we have such pleasure from it? In what part of ourselves do we experience this pleasure?

We ask questions, form our own answers and speculate endlessly. Perhaps music is a coded message which guides our souls endlessly through many successive lives. This is probably what Pythagoras and his followers believed. Perhaps one of the functions of music is to make us speculate in this way, because by asking questions we develop our awareness and consciousness of life. If so, it is all the more important that we listen to as many types of music as possible. Let's start listening today and never stop listening to and making music. Then, for each one of us, the mystery may be solved.

Dedicated to my daughter Kate and to Liz Greene,
both of whom in their unique ways helped me to
touch my own creativity.

With grateful thanks to Mary Verney, Professor of Harpsichord at the Guildhall School of Music and Dance for her help in checking the manuscript .

Graphics: Barry Dunnage.

Colour reproduction: Colour Workshop Ltd.

The Green Violinist (1923-4) by Marc Chagall with the permission of the Solomon R. Guggenheim Museum. New York.

The illustrations in the Instrument section are based on examples taken from *Musical Instruments of the World*, produced by the Diagram Group.